FIRST PEOPLES

THE INUIT

OF CANADA

DANIELLE CORRIVEAU

Lerner Publications Company • Minneapolis

**First American edition published in 2002
by Lerner Publications Company**

Published by arrangement with Times Editions

Copyright © 2002 by Times Media Private Limited

Lerner Publications Company
A division of Lerner Publishing Group
241 First Avenue North
Minneapolis, MN 55401 U.S.A.
Website address: www.lernerbooks.com

Series originated and designed by
Times Editions
An imprint of Times Media Private Limited
A member of the Times Publishing Group
1 New Industrial Road, Singapore 536196
Website address: www.timesone.com.sg/te

Series editors: Margaret J. Goldstein, Karen Kwek
Series designers: Tuck Loong, Sandy Sum
Series picture researcher: Susan Jane Manuel

Library of Congress Cataloging-in-Publication Data
Corriveau, Danielle.
The Inuit of Canada / by Danielle Corriveau.
p. cm. — (First peoples)
Includes bibliographical references and index.
ISBN 0-8225-4850-X (lib. bdg. : alk. paper)
1. Inuit—Juvenile literature. [1. Inuit. 2. Eskimos.] I. Title. II. Series.
E99.E7 C738 2002
971.9004'9712—dc21   00-012183

Printed in Singapore
Bound in the United States of America

1 2 3 4 5 6—0S—07 06 05 04 03 02

CONTENTS

THE INUIT OF THE ARCTIC

The name *Inuit*, meaning "the people," refers to native people who live in the Arctic North, specifically in Canada, Alaska, Greenland, and the Russian Far East. For ten thousand years, the Inuit have survived in one of the coldest regions on earth. The modern Inuit number more than one hundred thousand. They traditionally lived in small groups, or bands, that were scattered over hundreds of thousands of square miles. Modern Inuit people generally live in small towns. In 1999, a separate Inuit territory was created in northwestern Canada. This territory, Nunavut, is home to many Canadian Inuit.

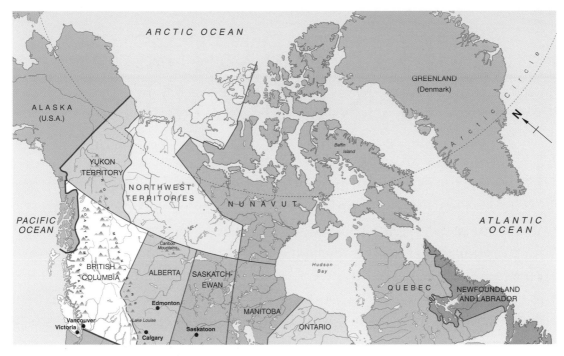

Different Groups

The Inuit people are divided into many different groups. The divisions are based on where people live and on their traditional languages. Inuit groups from Greenland and the islands north of Canada are sometimes called the Archipelago Inuit. The term Barrengrounds Inuit is sometimes used to describe groups in mainland Canada and in Alaska. In earlier times, the Archipelago Inuit survived by hunting seals and whales. A group often would stay on one island for several years before traveling to find better hunting grounds. The Barrengrounds Inuit were traditionally nomadic (traveling) hunters. They followed caribou from the Arctic coast in summer, south to the edge of the forests in winter, then back north again in spring.

LOTS OF NAMES

European explorers, arriving in Inuit lands in the 1500s, called the Inuit "Eskimos." That was a name used by neighboring Indians, not by the Inuit themselves. Historians once thought that *Eskimo* meant "eaters of raw flesh," but current scholars think the name probably refers to snowshoes. The Inuit in Canada are no longer called Eskimos, although Inuit in Alaska (*right*) often use the name. In general, Inuit people prefer names based on their traditional regions and languages. Some regional names include Inupiat in northern Alaska and Yupik in Russia and southwestern Alaska.

THE ARCTIC LANDSCAPE

The Inuit live near the Arctic Circle, where the sun doesn't set for several months in summer and doesn't rise for several months in winter. This freezing land is too cold for many kinds of plants and animals. Evergreen forests grow south of the Arctic. The northern edge of the forests is called the tree line. North of this line, the climate is too cold for trees.

Storms in the Arctic

Parts of the Arctic receive less than 10 inches (25 centimeters) of rainfall a year, and the air holds very little moisture. As fierce winds blow over the ice and snow, they pick up tiny, loose ice crystals. Arctic snowstorms can blow so much snow and ice around that it becomes impossible to see anything ahead. This kind of storm is called a whiteout.

Right: North of the tree line, the landscape is carved by wind and frost.

As Seasons Change

During winter, Arctic temperatures can fall to -40 degrees Fahrenheit (-40 degrees Celsius) and lower. With long cold winters and short cool summers, only the very top of the ground ever thaws. The frozen part beneath is called permafrost. Permafrost keeps water from draining into the ground, even during the summer thaw. Because of the permafrost, parts of the Arctic turn into squishy bogs (stretches of wet ground) every summer. Another name for this bog is muskeg.

Above: Arctic cotton grass grows on the muskeg in summer.

LIGHTS IN THE SKY

The aurora borealis, or northern lights (*below*), can sometimes be seen in the Arctic night sky. Created by electrically charged particles from the sun, the lights dance across the sky in huge colored bands, ribbons, and flashes. The most common colors are white, green, pink, and red. The northern lights are best seen in winter in far northern regions, although they sometimes appear in summer as well. Inuit legend says that the lights are ancestors coming down to visit their relatives in the Arctic.

A FROZEN WORLD

Throughout the year, pack ice (ice floes and icebergs) floats through the Arctic Ocean. Floes are large sheets of floating ice, with the biggest measuring more than 10 miles (16 kilometers) across. Icebergs are giant chunks of ice that break off the ends of glaciers (large sheets of moving ice that once covered much of the region).

Pack Ice and Coastal Ice

Ice floes can push against and on top of each other with tremendous force, creating ridges of ice as tall as 20 feet (6 meters) or more. In summer, the floes melt only partway, leaving sharp spears and edges called candled ice. It is difficult to walk on this ice because it can cut through boots and into the skin.

Above: Ice floes push up against one another.

Unlike ice floes and icebergs, coastal ice is frozen to the land and stays put. Because of all the ice, waves can't wash directly against the land, creating sandy beaches. Instead, the beaches of the Arctic consist mainly of pebbles and rocks.

Right: Groups of ice floes and icebergs sometimes jam and freeze together to form giant ice islands.

Moraines and Eskers

The Arctic mainland includes features left by glaciers. Low, flat-topped hills called moraines mark areas where glaciers stopped and melted. Moraines are actually huge piles of rock and gravel (a mixture of pebbles and other small stones) that the glaciers crunched and then dumped as they moved slowly over the land. Eskers, long low ridges, mark the spots where rivers once flowed from beneath melting glaciers. Between the eskers, moraines, and coastlines stretch the vast distances of the Arctic tundra.

Above: Many rivers and lakes carved out by glaciers mark the tundra.

ICEBERG FORMATION

As snow piles up on a glacier every winter, it pushes the glacier forward. Once the glacier reaches the coast, huge pieces break off and fall into the sea. The sound of glaciers breaking can be heard for miles around. The fallen pieces of ice are called icebergs (*below*). The process by which they break off and fall is known as calving.

ARCTIC VEGETATION

Plants in the Arctic have adapted to extreme weather by growing close to the ground, so fierce winds can't blow them down. Many of these plants look stunted and bent or twisted, very different from plants that grow in warmer regions to the south.

Survival Strategies

Above: The arctic willow tree can live to be hundreds of years old.

The arctic willow, if it were not bent, might be up to 60 feet (18 meters) tall. Instead, it is only a few inches tall. It grows spread out over the ground, covering up to 50 square feet (4.5 square meters). It has much thicker bark than willow trees that grow to the south, and its leaves are a deeper green in summer. The weather is so cold that the arctic willow's sap runs for only about sixty days of the year.

Above: The flowers of the arctic poppy rotate with the sun during the day to "catch" the most sunlight.

Plants have adapted to Arctic conditions by using the long daylight hours in summer to their advantage and growing very fast. After the snow melts at the end of winter, the arctic poppy grows from a seed into a foot-tall (30-centimeter-tall) plant, which blooms and then produces more seeds, in a matter of weeks. Some of these seeds will survive and grow into plants the next summer.

Above: Lichen covers a rock, and wildflowers bloom in summer.

Hardy Plants

Grasses of all kinds grow well in the Arctic. Wildflowers carpet the valleys every summer. The grasses are important food for animals such as caribou and musk oxen. The Inuit, too, once used grasses for fuel, as lining for boots and clothing, and as floor mats for summer tents.

The summer daylight is perfect for plants such as lichens and mosses. They grow in dense clusters during the many hours of sunlight. Grouping together for protection allows them to survive extremely well long after other plants have withered and died for the year.

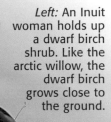

Left: An Inuit woman holds up a dwarf birch shrub. Like the arctic willow, the dwarf birch grows close to the ground.

USEFUL PLANTS

A silvery gray lichen called caribou moss, or tripe-de-roche, is found throughout the Arctic in large quantities. It is a main winter food for caribou, and was also a very important plant for the Inuit. When animals were scarce, the Inuit survived by eating this lichen. Mosses (*below*) were also very important to the Inuit, who originally used them to make wicks for lamps and diapers for babies.

ANIMALS ON LAND AND IN THE SEA

A lmost everything the Inuit needed to live, from clothes and tools to food and fuel, came from the animals of the Arctic.

Above: The harp seal pup is born with a fluffy white coat.

Seals and Whales

Seals spend much of their lives in the water. As the ocean freezes, they make breathing holes in the ice, breaking it with their heads. They swim from one hole to another under the ice and can stay underwater for as long as twenty minutes. When blizzards blow above them, seals are perfectly content to stay in the water, kept warm by layers of fat beneath their skin.

Several kinds of whales swim in the Arctic, including the white beluga, the orca (killer whale), and the narwhal. The Inuit hunt bowhead and gray whales for food.

Walruses

Like seals but much larger, walruses are sea animals that live together in herds. Each bull, or male walrus, protects its cows and calves (females and children) from polar bears and orcas with its long tusks.

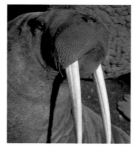

Above: A male walrus can weigh up to 3,000 pounds (1,365 kilograms).

Caribou and Musk Oxen

Caribou are herd animals that travel thousands of miles in their annual migration. Both males and females have long curved, forked antlers.

Musk oxen have long thick hair that helps them survive the cold. When threatened, the adults will form a ring around their calves, with their heads out, ready to ram intruders. The Inuit hunt caribou and musk oxen for their skin and meat.

Arctic Foxes

The arctic fox is prized for its shiny white winter coat. Its feet are covered with fur for warmth and for good grip on slippery, icy surfaces.

Left: Gray or brown in summer, the coat of the arctic fox turns white in winter.

Polar Bears

The most famous of Arctic predators is the polar bear. At the shoulder, it's almost as tall as a human (5 feet/1.5 meters), and its razor-sharp claws can measure up to 6 inches (15 centimeters) in length. The polar bear's favorite food is the seal. Bears that live near Hudson Bay travel on land in summer, but those in the islands farther north stay on the ice pack all year. It takes a mother bear two years to raise a cub, and she may give birth (usually to twin cubs) every other year.

Below: Polar bears have an excellent sense of smell, sharp teeth, super strength, and lightning quickness.

BUG COUNTRY

Every summer, vast clouds of mosquitoes and blackflies fill the waterlogged tundra. The insects are so numerous that even large animals can bleed to death from their bites. When the air is thick with mosquitoes, caribou will run many miles to escape them. Birds from all over North America migrate to the Arctic in summer to feed on the insects and to breed.

INUIT ANCESTORS

Experts believe the ancestors of the Inuit migrated (traveled) to North America on foot. They followed game over the Bering Land Bridge. This strip of land connected Asia and North America about ten thousand years ago and has since been covered by water.

Ancient Arctic Peoples

Some experts think that the ancestors of the Inuit may have come from mainland Asia. Other evidence suggests that they came from Japan and other islands along the northern Pacific coast. They might have journeyed to the Bering Land Bridge in coracles, skin-covered boats similar to modern Inuit umiaks. The North American Arctic offered rich hunting grounds, and the newcomers chose to stay.

Experts refer to one early Inuit group as the Dorset culture. Their tools and possessions were made of bone, driftwood, and sometimes stone. The Dorset people left little behind, except for the remains of large oval houses, dug into pebbly beaches. Later Inuit groups kept many of the Dorset people's ideas and inventions. But the Dorset culture itself disappeared about seven hundred years ago. Nobody knows why.

Above: Archaeologists examine evidence of ancient cultures in Alaska.

The Thule Culture

Modern Inuit people are descended from a culture known as the Thule. This group spread eastward from Alaska to Greenland, where they were first described by Scandinavian explorers. The Thule people used

Above: An ancient qiliq found on Baffin Island

dogsleds, kayaks, and umiaks for both hunting and travel. Thule tools were more elaborately decorated and carved than were Dorset tools. They included many figures and symbols not seen on Dorset instruments. Both the Dorset and the Thule made soapstone items like the qiliq, a kind of lamp.

Above: Early whale hunters in Alaska used kayaks to travel on water.

Left: The whalebone frames of ancient Thule dwellings have been found in Resolute Bay, Canada.

THE COPPER ESKIMOS

After his first stay in the Arctic, American anthropologist and explorer Vilhjalmur Stefansson announced to the world in 1910 that he had found a "new kind of Eskimo." Stefansson called the group (*below*) Copper Eskimos because they used local supplies of copper to make tools. He was quite sure that he had found the descendants of the lost Dorset culture. It turned out, however, that the Copper Eskimos were Barrengrounds Inuit. The only difference between them and other Inuit groups was that they lived in such a remote part of Canada that they had never before met any white people.

NEWCOMERS TO THE ARCTIC

The earliest outsiders to the Inuit world were the Vikings, sailors from Iceland and Norway, who established a settlement on Greenland in A.D. 985. The Vikings called the Inuit *skraelings*, meaning "rough people" or "savages" because they thought they were very frightening. This was because the Inuit were hunters, and they carried their tools—harpoons, spears, and bows—with them all the time.

Left: Vikings arrived in Greenland in the late tenth century.

The Viking Settlement

The Vikings soon realized that the Inuit were very friendly. Inuit people showed them what to eat, how to dress, and how to build houses for protection from the cold. In the 1300s, the climate turned colder. For about three hundred years, no ships could pass through the frozen Davis Strait, on Greenland's southwest coast. By the time European ships arrived in Greenland again around 1600, the Viking group had vanished. Modern experts aren't sure why. Some think harsh weather and attacks by the Inuit might have killed the Vikings. Others think the Vikings might have abandoned the settlement and adopted the Inuit way of life.

Frobisher's Gold

Above:
Martin Frobisher

In 1576, Englishman Martin Frobisher was the first European to arrive on Baffin Island, northeast of Hudson Bay. He had set out in search of the Northwest Passage, a water route across the Arctic to Asia. Along the way, Frobisher thought he had found gold on Baffin Island. He also clashed with the local Inuit. He kidnapped some Inuit men and left five of his own men behind on the island. The Inuit tell stories of how these men tried to build a boat and sail home but ended up starving and freezing to death. Back in England, Frobisher's "gold" turned out to be a much less valuable rock called mica.

Whalers and Fur Traders

In the 1600s, Europeans went to the Arctic to hunt whales for whale oil, which was used to make lantern fuel, candles, and other products. European whalers also brought home the beautiful white fur of the arctic fox. Attracted by reports of fabulous beaver and fox furs, English merchants founded the Hudson's Bay Company in 1670. Every year, the company sent men to Southampton Island, in the north of the bay, to get furs from the Inuit. After 1800, the company started setting up trading posts so that the Inuit and the traders did not have so far to travel to meet each other.

Left: In the 1600s, Europeans arrived in the Arctic to hunt whales.

THE FIRST INUIT TOWNS

The Hudson's Bay Company saw the Canadian Arctic as a commercial empire and at first did not allow European settlers or missionaries (religious workers) to enter the region. The traders became the only source for goods that the Inuit got from the outside world. They bought furs from the Inuit and sold them food, clothing, tools, and other manufactured products. They sometimes protected the Inuit from dishonest whalers, explorers, and other outsiders. The Inuit came to depend on their relationship with the company and began to settle around the trading posts. These posts became the first permanent Inuit villages.

IN SEARCH OF THE NORTHWEST PASSAGE

I n the early 1800s, many people became interested in traveling to unexplored parts of the world. New shipbuilding technology made long sea voyages possible. More explorers set off to the Arctic, again hoping to find the Northwest Passage.

Above: For many years, parties searched for Franklin in the Arctic.

Some Early Explorers

The English government offered a lot of prize money to the first person to sail the passage from one end to the other. Between 1818 and 1833, explorers John Ross and William Parry each made several voyages to the Arctic, but they could not get their ships through the ice. In I845, John Franklin accepted the challenge, taking with him 129 men, two ships, and enough food for five years. The entire party died, but for many years no one in England knew their fate. A search party found the remains of some crew members, along with a written record from the ship, in 1859.

There were more tragedies like Franklin's, partly because the explorers failed to adopt Inuit methods of survival in the harsh climate. The Inuit ate lots of vitamin-rich raw meat, but the explorers had a poor diet of salted and cooked meat without vegetables. The Inuit dressed in warm sealskins and furs, but the explorers wore woolen uniforms, which could not keep out the cold.

Success!

American Elisha Kent Kane was the first explorer to learn from the Inuit. He dressed in parkas and mukluks (sealskin boots) and ate the same food that the Inuit did. In the 1850s, he and his team successfully mapped a large part of the Arctic.

The Northwest Passage was finally sailed from end to end by Roald Amundsen, a Norwegian, in his small ship *Gjoa* in 1906.

Below: Members of John Ross's 1829–1833 expedition to the Arctic met local Inuit people.

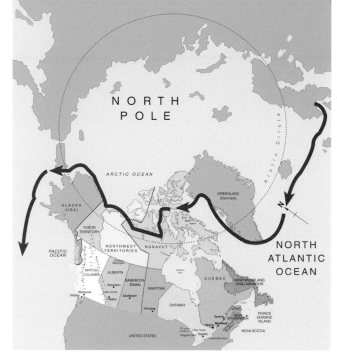

Above: Amundsen's route. The Northwest Passage turned out to be useless for shipping—it was too shallow and full of ice to allow large boats to pass through.

MURDER MYSTERY

An Ohio businessman named Charles Francis Hall was so moved by the disappearance of John Franklin that he went looking for him and "found" the Inuit instead. He befriended an Inuit couple (*right*) and lived with them on Baffin Island for fifteen years. In 1871, the U.S. government sent Hall to search for the North Pole. He died of arsenic poisoning during the expedition, and some suspect he was murdered by someone on his crew. Despite an investigation into Hall's death, the murder remains a mystery.

GREAT CHANGES

After Canadian confederation—the union of British colonies to form Canada in 1867—most of the land owned by the Hudson's Bay Company was transferred to Canada. The Inuit who lived on this land came under the protection of the Canadian government.

Canada's Mounties

To establish control in its new territory, the government established Royal Canadian Mounted Police (RCMP) outposts throughout the Canadian Arctic. The Mounties took over many of the duties that the Hudson's Bay Company had performed before confederation.

Hardship and Diseases

Along with other European settlers, missionaries came to Canada. They wanted to convert the Inuit, who practiced their own traditional religion, to Christianity. The missionaries took some Inuit children away from their families, to boarding schools run by the church. There, the children were not allowed to speak their native languages or to practice Inuit traditions. The Europeans also brought with them diseases such as smallpox, measles, and tuberculosis, which killed many Inuit people.

Left: Christian Inuit leaders. European missionaries brought Christianity to the Inuit.

Modernizing

By the early 1900s, fewer and fewer Inuit knew how to make their living by hunting and trapping. Some moved to towns and cities to take paying jobs. Many others lived in poverty, unable to find work. In the 1950s, the Canadian government tried to create a list of all Inuit people in order to provide them with government-sponsored education

Above: From the 1950s onward, the towns around Hudson's Bay Company trading posts grew larger.

and medical care. To get these services, many Inuit had to move to central locations around Hudson's Bay Company trading posts.

Industry also arrived in the Arctic, as companies came to mine coal, drill for oil, and extract other natural resources. But still, few jobs were available to the Inuit. Many Inuit people had little education and thus were unqualified for high-paying jobs.

Left: Established in the 1870s, the Royal Canadian Mounted Police are known as Mounties.

THE DEW LINE

The United States and the Soviet Union were allies during World War II (1939–1945). But after the war, distrust grew between the two countries because both had powerful weapons. Each feared the other might attack. In the 1950s, the United States and Canada jointly established the DEW (Distant Early Warning) line. This series of radar stations (*above*) stretched across the Arctic to keep watch for an attack from the Soviet Union. Some Inuit people took jobs helping to build and operate the system.

NUNAVUT: "OUR LAND"

The push for a better life for the Inuit in Canada began in 1972. The Canadian prime minister, Pierre Trudeau, published a paper calling for equal rights for minorities in Canada, including the Inuit. In the 1970s, the Inuit and the Canadian government began working toward creating a separate territory run by Inuit. After many years, special elections were held in 1992, leading to the official creation of Nunavut seven years later.

About Nunavut

Nunavut is a vast territory in northeastern Canada with mostly Inuit inhabitants. Its name means "Our Land" in the Inuit language.

Covering an area of about 733,600 square miles (1,900,000 square kilometers), Nunavut borders the Canadian province of Manitoba to the south and the Northwest Territories to the northwest and west. The Arctic Ocean lies to the north, Greenland to the northeast, and the Atlantic Ocean and Quebec to the east.

About 27,500 people live in Nunavut. Of this number, more than 20,000 are Inuit. The capital, Iqaluit, is the largest community in the eastern Canadian Arctic.

Right: An Inuit man waves the Nunavut flag in Iqaluit, the capital.

Governing Nunavut

The Nunavut government, run mostly by Inuit people, began operating in 1999. Nunavut has no political parties. The Inuit people elect a legislative (lawmaking) assembly, which rules by consensus. The nineteen members of the assembly choose their own premier (leader). On April 1, 1999, lawyer Paul Okalik was sworn in as the first premier of Nunavut.

Above: Nunavut premier Paul Okalik (seated) signed the Declaration of Celebration, marking the birth of Nunavut on April 1, 1999.

Preserving Traditions

When Christian missionaries took Inuit children to boarding schools, a lot of traditional knowledge was lost. But schools established in Arctic towns in recent years have begun to teach Inuit languages and traditional ways. In some Canadian schools, a Council of Elders teaches Inuit children how to live on the land, hunt, fish, and make snow houses and mukluks. In some schools, Inuit children can go out on the land for three weeks at a time with their elders and learn the old ways as part of their schoolwork.

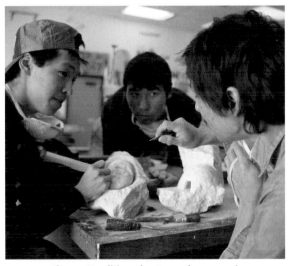

Above: Traditional arts such as carving are taught in modern schools.

THE FLAG OF NUNAVUT

The flag of Nunavut features a red inukshuk centered on a gold and white background. In the top right corner of the flag is a blue star. The inukshuk is a personlike structure that guides Inuit people on the land and marks special places. The colors gold and blue represent the riches of the land, sea, and sky in Nunavut. Red stands for Canada. The star represents the North Star, the brightest in the Northern Hemisphere. The star symbolizes constancy, or the quality of always remaining the same.

SHARING THE ABUNDANCE

Traditional Inuit society had no money. Everything necessary for life came from the land and the water, and everyone had equal access to all of it. Every member of a band shared the work, doing whatever he or she did best. Everyone in the band also shared in the rewards of one another's work.

Items for All

Originally all food came from the hunt. Afterward, the Inuit gathered round and ate their meat raw, preferably before it was frozen solid. The food belonged to everyone equally, and it was shared among the entire band.

Some items belonged to everyone in the band or family but were cared for by just one person. For example, a strong woman usually looked after and pitched the tent, although the entire family used it. A hunter was usually in charge of the kumatik (sled) and the sled dogs.

Above: Taking charge of the kumatik

Belongings

Personal items, such as clothing and knives, were used too often to share. For instance, a knife was essential for every Inuit at mealtime. Each person would cut meat from an animal in a long narrow strip and then hold it in his or her teeth. The person would use a knife to slice off, rather than bite off, a mouthful. Items that were not in use were often put into a cache, or enclosure. Anyone who needed to use an item could borrow it, returning it to the cache later.

Above: A cache might be marked by an inukshuk, a pile of stones shaped like a person.

Below: An Inuit father and son show off their catch.

Beautiful Objects

The most beautiful and special things, like carvings and jewelry, were owned for only a short time. Then they were given away to anyone who expressed an interest in or admired them. Inuit people did not expect to possess such objects permanently. Often, items were given to visitors who brought other new and special objects to the band.

Above: An Inuit woman displays an ivory necklace.

OWNING A STORY

Some nonphysical things also were considered property. For instance, stories belonged to the first person to tell them. No one could repeat a story unless the owner sold it or exchanged it for something else. Nobody would listen to a stolen story. By exchanging stories for food or goods, a talented storyteller with a good imagination could survive without ever having to hunt at all!

CHANGING TRADITIONS

The idea of trade is a very old one among the Inuit. While all the things necessary for life were available to all people alike in the Arctic, some special things came from outside. The modern Inuit economy is a combination of old and new ways of life.

Furs for Weapons

The Archipelago Inuit traded with the Vikings of the Greenland colonies and with whalers. The Barrengrounds Inuit traded actively with the nearby Dene Indians. After Europeans arrived in the Arctic, the Inuit traded animal furs for guns and metal knives, which made hunting much easier. However, fur trapping took time away from hunting, and as hunting decreased, the Inuit were forced to rely more and more on outside sources of food. With the end of the fur trade in the 1900s, the Inuit faced economic disaster. Many fell into poverty, and some were forced to live on welfare.

Above: Furs are displayed for sale in an Arctic shop.

Right: An Inuit man repairs his sled using modern power tools.

Combining Old and New

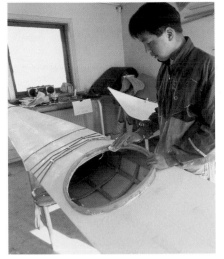

Above: A kayak maker uses modern materials.

Modern Inuit still rely on hunting, fishing, sharing, and trading for their needs. But they combine these old traditions with modern products and a cash system. For example, an Inuit might go seal hunting with a rifle instead of a harpoon. He may then give some of his catch to a relative, who had given him money to fix his snowmobile the winter before. The hunter also gives some seal meat to a single mom, who will repay the favor by making him a caribou-hide parka. He takes the rest of the meat home to his parents, and a neighbor stops by around dinnertime for some seal soup. In this way, the whole community shares in his hunting success.

Modern Jobs

In recent years, Inuit people have started new businesses, such as native arts and handicraft stores, the Inuit Broadcasting Corporation in Canada, and several airlines. Many Inuit people also work in the mining industry and as government employees. Tourism is another source of income. Many Inuit people have found work as tour guides, hotel clerks, and cooks.

Above: An Arctic tour bus

GOING "GREEN"

Underground stores of oil and natural gas lie beneath the Arctic Ocean. Many people hope the oil and gas industry will provide jobs to the Inuit. But the risks must be carefully studied. The Arctic environment is so delicate that it can take years for wildlife to recover from industrial disasters such as oil spills. Some Inuit have found jobs protecting the environment.

SNOW HOUSES AND TENT HOUSES

When people think of the Inuit, they think of igloos—domes made of snow. But not all Inuit houses were made of snow, and snow houses differed widely.

Above: A tourist sits inside a snow house.

Igloos

The most common snow house was the single-family dome. It was built to last a few months and was replaced only when it got very dirty. Inside the igloo, the central dome held a snow platform on one end, opposite the tunnel that served as the igloo door. The igloo tunnel was built below floor level, to help keep warm air inside the home from escaping. The family slept and ate on the platform, which was covered with a layer of furs.

A small shelf on one side of the platform held the qiliq, a lamp made of soapstone and used to heat the igloo. A hide placed fur-side-up against the ceiling kept melting ice from dripping inside the home.

Sometimes, several families built snow houses close together, with individual houses linked by tunnels to a large central igloo. Everyone gathered in the large house to tell stories and to socialize. Families went to their own houses only to sleep.

Right: Snow houses were built strong enough to withstand the weight of a polar bear.

Tent Houses

In spring, the roofs of snow houses began to melt. The Inuit moved to dugout tent houses—oval pits dug into the gravel and dirt of a beach, with a tunnel on one end and a sleeping platform on the other. The walls were made of gravel and stones, with a driftwood crossbeam placed over the top. For a roof, hides were draped over the beam and weighted down with rocks. Grasses and moss formed the floor. In summer, regular tent houses were made much the same way as dugout ones. Center and surrounding poles supported a crossbeam. A ring of stones held down the tent cover, which was traditionally made of caribou skins.

Below: A traditional summer tent

HOW TO BUILD AN IGLOO

Although it looks hard to make, a snow house could be built in a couple of hours. First, the builders found snow that had been packed solid by the wind. Then they drew a circle in the snow, with the northern side set against a snowdrift, for protection from fierce northern winds. Using a long "snow knife," they cut blocks about 6 inches  (15 centimeters) wide, 6 inches thick, and 1 foot (30 centimeters) long from inside the circle. These blocks were placed in a ring around the circle. The blocks were then spiraled upward, with each additional layer of blocks tilting inward slightly toward the middle of the circle. From the outside, loose snow was packed between the blocks. Lastly, the top block, which was circular  instead of rectangular, was set in place from outside. The tunnel hole was cut into the south side of the igloo, and the tunnel was built with more snow blocks. Then a window of clear ice was placed above the tunnel. An igloo could be as big or as small as the builder wanted.

MODERN ARCTIC TOWNS

The Inuit no longer live in snow houses or tent houses, but modern Inuit houses are still designed to provide protection from bad weather. Modeled after Western-style houses, modern buildings in the Arctic are compact.

Above: A modern kitchen in an Inuit home

Homes

Like igloos, modern houses often have the northern side set against a slope and the door facing south. These features provide shelter against icy winds that blow from the north. The Inuit build their houses close to beaches and landings, so that supplies do not have to travel long distances. The houses are grouped close together, serving as windbreaks for one another. They are also small, because fuel is scarce in the Arctic and very expensive. A small house is easier and cheaper to keep warm. Unlike igloos, modern Inuit houses usually include plumbing, electrical systems, and central heating systems.

Pollution

Modern Inuit towns are generally located in valleys, which help protect people and homes from strong Arctic winds. Houses and vehicles clustered close together in valleys can create pollution, however. Sometimes, exhaust fumes and water vapor freeze in the air and create a thick cloud that hovers overhead for days at a time. This "arctic smog" or "arctic haze" is especially common in winter.

Above: Inuit houses in Arviat, Nunavut

Below: The town of Igloolik, Foxe Basin, Nunavut

THE OLD TRADING POSTS

The first permanent houses in the Arctic were the Hudson's Bay Company trading posts. They became the model for other Arctic buildings, such as medical clinics and schools. The trading posts usually had the same basic design. Behind the store portion of the building, where people bought and sold goods, were two more rooms—a living room and a kitchen. Upstairs was a sleeping loft for the trader and the assistants.

LIFE IN THE INUIT BAND

The traditional Inuit band, or small group, consisted of several families and sometimes friends. A child usually grew up in his or her parents' band. But if the child needed to learn a skill that nobody in the band knew, he or she might go to live with an aunt and uncle's band to learn the skill as an apprentice, or trainee. Sometimes, an elder would take a child from another band as a helper and would teach the child practical skills in return. Families sometimes moved from one band to another, too.

Above: Inuit elders are greatly respected for their experience.

The Leader Knew Best

Everyone in the band got a say in group activities and how they would be done. A good hunter or the captain of a whaling boat might be considered the leader of the band. But he was really only the boss of what he knew best. Nobody, not even a leader or elder, could force another person to do something his or her way. There were no penalties for disobeying the leader.

Men's and Women's Jobs

Men and women each had their own jobs. For instance, men were the hunters, and women made clothing. But men and women knew enough about each other's jobs to be able to take over in an emergency. If a man could not hunt because of an injury or an illness, a woman would trap or shoot dinner instead.

Left: An Inuit woman chews on a piece of animal hide to soften it for sewing gloves.

Children's Lives

Above: These Inuit boys are taking care of puppies.

Inuit children's toys were usually small versions of adult tools. A girl might have a small needle as a toy, while a boy might use miniature weapons. Inuit children learned to take care of themselves at a young age. Adults always listened to children, although they didn't always agree with them. Inuit children were considered adults when they showed that they could look after themselves. A boy became an adult by hunting and killing an animal. He would bring his first kill to his mother and invite all the adults to the feast. A girl might choose to make a whole outfit for someone, usually a brother or father.

Left: Seal hunters haul their catch over the snow.

ARGUING INUIT-STYLE

When a small group of people live very close together and have to depend on each other for survival, anger can be a problem. The Inuit traditionally avoided arguing with each other, and they tried not to carry grudges. Instead, they used ritual to deal with angry feelings. When someone was upset with another person, he or she announced it to everyone else. Both people got ready, then held a story time. The angry person told everyone in the band what was wrong but had to do so by joking. The other person then got to defend him or herself, also using humor. The winner of the "argument" was the one who made everyone laugh the hardest.

TRAVELING IN THE ARCTIC

The Arctic environment looks much the same over large stretches of land, so the Inuit are very good at remembering details about the land. They are also good at reading the landscape. Snowdrifts show the wind direction and help them locate home. People know that clouds over open water or land are dark. Light-colored clouds indicate snow or ice floes below.

On Water

Kayaks and umiaks were used for traveling on open water in summer. Kayaks, narrow covered boats, held one person, while umiaks were big open boats that held six or even eight people, along with all their baggage and tools. Both types of boats were made of sealskin stretched over wooden frames.

Above: Kayaks were traditionally made by women but were used only by men. Women used umiaks.

Right: Dogs hitched in a fan formation pull a kumatik.

All Kinds of Transportation

Even in modern times, there are few permanent roads in the Arctic. Yet journeys of more than 1,000 miles (1,600 kilometers) are not uncommon. The modern Inuit use powered vehicles such as motorboats, all-terrain vehicles, and snowmobiles. Cars, trucks, and motorbikes are usually used only within towns. These vehicles require expensive fuel, which has to be brought in from the south. Many Inuit people still use dog teams. Dogs are more reliable and less expensive to maintain than snowmobiles.

Above: Many modern Inuit own snowmobiles.

Over Ice and Snow

Traveling was best done in winter, when the kumatik and dog teams could run over the snow and ice. A kumatik was made of animal bone and driftwood tied together. This construction made the sled loose and flexible and easy to drive over rough ice and snow.

COURAGEOUS BUSH PILOTS

In modern times, the airplane (*above*) is the most important vehicle in the Arctic. Besides getting travelers from one town to another quickly, airplanes function as ambulances and search-and-rescue vehicles. The weather in the Arctic often makes flying very difficult, however. Arctic pilots, or bush pilots as they are better known, are famous for getting planes into and out of dangerous landing sites, small places, and even blizzards and fog. Without the courage and skill of the bush pilots who provide essential services year-round, the Arctic would be a much less accessible and more dangerous place.

THE WARMEST CLOTHING ON EARTH

O ver the centuries, the Inuit grew very skilled at living in their frozen world. In fact, their way of dressing for the cold has not been improved, even with modern materials and technology.

Above: The basic parts of the Inuit outfit were an inner tunic, a parka, pants, leggings worn over the pants, mukluks, and gloves.

Keeping Out the Cold

Traditionally, all Inuit clothing was made from animal skins and furs. In the archipelago region, sealskin, which is waterproof, was the most common and practical choice. On the Barrengrounds, caribou hide was the most common fabric. Clothing was usually made with the animal's fur or hair on the inside, next to the body. This way, the fur trapped air and kept the person warm no matter how cold it was outside.

Parkas and Tunics

In summer, people wore light inner tunics made of bird skins. In winter, they wore thick tunics woven from strips of fur. The parka was a large coat made all in one piece (without a front opening). It would be pulled down over the head and tied around the waist.

Right: A woman's parka has a large and deep hood, used by a mother to carry a baby on her back.

Mukluks and Accessories

Leggings, mukluks, and gloves were made with the fur side out, so that snow and ice could be easily shaken off. Several pouches hung from a belt around the waist. Made from the skins of small animals, the pouches held tools, knives, and other small items. Eye protection is important in the Arctic because when the sun shines on snow, the glare can cause temporary blindness.

Above: Mukluks keep feet warm, even when walking on snow.

Modern science has improved upon one Inuit item—snow goggles. Old-style goggles were round wooden disks pierced by narrow slits. They blocked excess light but limited the wearer's vision. Modern snow goggles and sunglasses cut the glare but leave the field of vision wide open.

Modern Materials

Modern Inuit people sometimes wear parkas made of wool, covered with a windproof nylon shell. However, the trim on such parkas is still made of animal fur. Artificial fur absorbs moisture from the wearer's breath and then freezes to the skin. Some modern synthetic fabrics keep a person dry but let the wind through. Others keep the wind out while making the wearer perspire. Both cases can result in frostbite (injury to any body part exposed to extreme cold). Animal skins reduce perspiration and keep out icy winds at the same time.

FABULOUS FABRICS

Traditional Inuit clothing was beautifully decorated (*right*). Embroidery, fur and leather patchwork, and sometimes beadwork all were used to decorate clothing, and each clothing maker had a unique style. Glass beads (obtained through trade) were very precious items on clothing, since nothing in the Inuit environment looked quite like them. Designs on clothing included fantastic flowers, animals and birds, and scenes of Inuit life.

ARCTIC CRAFTS

The first rule of the Inuit artist is to use the materials at hand. Craftspeople use serpentine, soapstone, ivory, bone, and driftwood to make beautiful carvings. Some carvings are simple pieces with flowing lines and few details. Others are detailed, lifelike sculptures. Subjects include animals and birds, scenes from everyday life, and portraits of individuals.

Carved Objects

Even everyday objects are sometimes elaborately carved. A knife handle might be carved specially to fit a hand and also decorated with symbols and patterns. Generally, carving is an ongoing activity. The longer an item stays with a carver, the more decorated it becomes. The item is considered finished only when it is given away.

Right: An Inuit sculptor works on his newest piece.

Pictures and Drawings

Inuit pictures sometimes take the form of outlines cut from scraps of fur or hide. These story-pictures are often displayed on the wall of a snow house and are used to help tell stories. Other pictures are drawn directly into sand or snow outdoors. A drawing might be extremely complex, with lines blending and repeating and many parts of a story contained within the patterns. Elaborate drawings are most often made on bags and packs, and sometimes on clothing and walls.

Above: In this Inuit work, figures cut from fabric have been stitched onto a cloth backing.

Paintings and Prints

Above: An Inuit printmaker displays her work.

Painting and printing have become popular among modern Inuit artists. Traditional Inuit design lends itself easily to printmaking in particular. An advantage of modern housing is that central heating systems keep paints and inks from freezing. Modern Inuit paintings often include the same elements and designs as traditional story-pictures. Many modern Inuit artists have combined methods from Western schools of art with traditional forms. The works of Inuit artists are widely shown in museums and galleries the world over, not just in Arctic areas.

STITCHING AND WEAVING

Inuit women were proud of their needlework. A girl aimed to make stitches as fine as her mother's—quite an achievement when the needle was made of bone and the fabric was animal skin! The arrival of the Europeans influenced Inuit needlework. They introduced threads in fabulous colors, needles of steel, crochet hooks, knitting needles, and looms for weaving. Boarding schools taught many Inuit girls the craft of weaving (*right*). In many Inuit villages, the town loom was the social center, where women gathered to chat, laugh, and create beautiful clothes, blankets, and wall hangings.

INUIT LANGUAGES

Traditionally, Inuit people in different regions spoke different languages. In Canada, for instance, Inuktitut was spoken in the archipelago region, while Barrengrounds people spoke Inuvialuit. Lots of words have the same meanings in both languages, but they are often pronounced differently. In modern times, many Inuit people speak English as well as their traditional language.

A "Right-Hand Language"

The Inuit call English a "left-hand language," because in English descriptive words come before a noun. An example is "black cat." Inuit languages switch the order to "cat black." In another example from the Inuit language, *inu* means "person," *inukshuk* means "personlike," and *inuktitut* means "person talking." The Inuit call their system a "right-hand language."

Right: An Inuit teacher shows her student the Inuit writing system.

Unusual Sounds

The Inuit languages have some sounds that are unfamiliar to English speakers. The most common one is represented by the letter *q*. It sounds a bit like a *k* sound, but stopped and "swallowed" instead. Inuit words can also have different meanings, depending on whether they are pronounced in a high or a low tone.

a	◁	u	▷	i	△	p	<
pa	<	pu	>	pi	Λ	p	<
ta	⊂	tu	⊃	ti	∩	t	⊂
ka	b	ku	d	ki	ρ	k	b
ga	L	gu	J	gi	ſ	g	L
ma	L	mu	⌐	mi	Γ	m	L
na	ᑫ	nu	ᖆ	ni	σ	n	ᒥ
sa	ᐟ	su	ᒧ	si	ᒃ	s	ᐟ
la	⊂	lu	⊃	li	⊏	l	ᒃ
ja	ᔭ	ju	ᔪ	ji	ᔨ	j	ᔾ
va	ᕙ	vu	ᕗ	vi	ᕕ	v	ᕝ
ra	ᖅ	ru	ᖁ	ri	ᖕ	r	ᕐ
qa	ᖅᑉ	qu	ᖅᑯ	qi	ᖅᑭ	q	ᖅᑉ
nga	ᖕᑉ	ngu	ᖖ	ngi	ᖏ	ng	ᖕ
&a	ᖧ	&u	ᖨ	&i	⊏	&	ᖦ

Above: The sound for each Inuit symbol is to the left of the symbol. The & represents a soft "dsl" sound that doesn't occur in English.

The Writing System

Experts believe modern Inuit languages come from Thule languages. Originally, the Inuit languages were only spoken. The Inuit did not have a written language. When missionaries came to Canada in the 1800s, they made up a writing system for Inuktitut and other Inuit languages.

OOTUKAHKUKTUVIK
"PLACE HAVING OLD THINGS"

LONG WORDS

English sentences are made up of separate words. In the Inuit languages, speakers add descriptions to root words to form extremely long words that contain whole phrases or sentences. An example is *ootukahkuktuvik* (*right*), which means "place having old things."

SPIRITS AND SKY PEOPLE

In modern times, many Inuit people practice Christianity. Traditionally the Inuit had their own religion. It was a very personal practice, not a group ritual. Instead of believing in heaven and God, the Inuit religion involved the relationship of each person to the spirits of the land and to life. This kind of religion, in which every place, every animal, every plant—everything in the world—has a spirit, is called animism.

Above: The Inuit believed that all people and animals take off their earthly skins when they die.

Sky People

The Inuit didn't believe in the idea of souls, life after death, heaven, and hell. In their religion, everything in the world always existed and always would. When a person or an animal died, according to Inuit belief, it took off the skin that it wore on earth and went to Summerland. There, the ancestors lived with the sky people— animals that were no longer wearing their skins.

Spirits of the World

The Inuit originally believed in spirits. Some of these spirits were friendly. Others disliked humans. Inuit people communicated with the spirits through shamans (people who had special spiritual powers).

In Inuit belief, the place that held things not yet born or created was called the void. It was a place of energy and magic, and a source of dreams, healing, and understanding. Dreams were very important to the Inuit. Every morning, everyone in the band would tell their dreams from the night before.

Shamans

The people who knew the most about Summerland, spirits, and the void were the shamans, called angekoks. They asked the spirits to show where animals were hiding, why someone was sick, or where something that was lost could be found. The shamans did not do any other kind of work and did not have their own households. They traveled from band to band. The Inuit respected shamans as the explainers of life but did not see them as leaders to be obeyed.

Below: The Inuit believed that **shamans** could tell them where to find animals for food.

THE LEGEND OF SEDNA

One of the most important spirits was Sedna (*above*), who was said to live under the ice and take care of all the animals that lived there. According to Inuit legend, Sedna was once a proud young woman who refused to marry. Her father pledged her to the next young man who arrived on their island, only to find out that he was a raven in disguise! When Sedna's father tried to rescue her from the raven's island, the bird chased his kayak out to sea and beat up a fierce storm with its wings. Terrified, Sedna's father threw her into the sea to save his own life. Sedna clung to the side of the kayak, but her father pounded at her hands until her frozen fingers fell off, turning into the first seals, walruses, and whales. Sedna sank beneath the waves. Because of her father's cruelty, she disliked all humans. The Inuit believed that if they were kind to Sedna, she would allow them to hunt her animals. But if an Inuit didn't pay attention to Sedna's lessons and knowledge, he or she would certainly have trouble when traveling over the ice floes on a dark winter night.

FUN AND GAMES

For the Inuit, survival depended entirely on knowing the land. The natural cycles in the Arctic are extreme. Knowing what to expect when was the key to survival. The changing seasons provided very good reasons to celebrate. But any event was a good excuse for a celebration, whether it was a boy's first hunt or two bands arriving in the same bay on the same day. A party would begin at once!

Celebrating the Seasons

During summer, the Inuit traditionally scattered and traveled all over the land. They fished, hunted, and enjoyed the long hours of daylight and the easy life of plentiful food.

As autumn arrived in the archipelago, and the days got shorter, bands met, and a celebration began. The feasting continued until the ice froze and the seals were again easy to hunt from the ice. To prepare for winter in the Barrengrounds, several bands of Inuit hunted together to kill a large number of caribou. Then there was another celebration, to thank the caribou for the meat and skins and to let them know how glad the people were to share life with them.

People kept the bladders of the seals killed in winter. In spring, they filled the bladders with air and floated them out to sea to thank Sedna for the catch and assure the seals a warm welcome the next winter.

Right: Inuit children play on melting ice floes in summer.

Party Games

Inuit parties always included lots of games. The favorites were games of chance. Every game had a prize, and everyone had a chance to win. Winning prizes was a way for people to share special items and to get a turn at "owning" something. Sometimes, a prize could change hands a dozen times during just one party. An item could always be won back at the next party.

Above: Lots of party games are still played outdoors.

Who's the Best?

Inuit celebrations, even small ones, often lasted for days. One way to keep things lively was to include lots of contests, with everything from races to knife-tossing competitions. The more skills someone demonstrated, the more interesting the contests became. Some competitions were wrestling matches. These matches showed fighting skills or settled disputes that couldn't be settled any other way.

MODERN SPORTS

Modern Inuit people like both team and individual sports. Ice hockey (*right*) is one of the most popular games in Canada, and every small Inuit settlement has a rink and a team. In Alaska, basketball is the most popular modern sport. In Greenland, people have revived the old hunting and kayaking skills and sometimes hold kayaking competitions. Dogsled racing is popular all over the Arctic, and many Inuit people are champion racers. Each year at the Arctic Winter Games, Inuit athletes compete in skiing, dogsled racing, snowshoeing, wrestling, and other contests.

GLOSSARY

angekok: an Inuit who had special powers to cure the sick or to find hidden things; a shaman

anthropologist: a scientist who studies the origins, lifestyles, and cultures of humankind

apprentice: someone who undergoes a period of training under an expert

archaeologist: a scientist who studies ancient cultures by analyzing their tools, crafts, and other remains

Arctic Circle: an imaginary line drawn parallel to the equator 1,624 miles south of the North Pole

bog: a stretch of wet, soggy ground

consensus: general agreement

glacier: a giant sheet of ice that moves slowly over the land

inukshuk (ee-NOOK-shook): a pile of stones, shaped like a person, used by the Inuit as a marker or signpost

kayak: a single-person boat, originally made of sealskin stretched over a wooden frame

kumatik (KOO-mah-tihk): an Inuit sled made of bone and wood

mukluks: sealskin boots

narwhal: a kind of whale. The male has a long tusk on its upper jaw.

nomadic: traveling from place to place, without a permanent home

Northwest Passage: a water route through the Arctic part of the North American continent. Many explorers sought the Northwest Passage in the 1800s.

permafrost: permanently frozen ground

predator: an animal that hunts and kills other animals for food

qiliq (GKEE-leegk): a soapstone lamp used to heat an Inuit home

serpentine: a green mineral or stone

shaman: *see angekok*

synthetic: artificial; manufactured

tree line: the line north of which the climate is too cold for trees to grow

tuberculosis: a disease of the lungs

tundra: a vast treeless plain that covers part of the Arctic region

umiak: a large wooden boat covered with animal skins

FINDING OUT MORE

Books

Finley, Carol. *Art of the Far North: Inuit Sculpture, Drawing, and Printmaking.* Minneapolis: Lerner Publications Company, 1998.

Hancock, Lyn. *Nunavut.* Minneapolis: Lerner Publications Company, 1995.

Mateer, Charlotte Ford, Louise Craft, and Linda Witt Fries. *Let's Go to the Arctic: A Story and Activities about Arctic People and Animals.* Boulder, CO: Roberts Rinehart Publishing, 1993.

Rootes, David. *The Arctic.* Minneapolis: Lerner Publications Company, 1996.

Smith, A. G., and Josie Hazen. *Inuit Punch-Out Masks.* Mineola, NY: Dover Publications, 1996.

Wallace, Mary. *The Inukshuk Book.* Toronto: Owl Communications, 1999.

Videos

Eyewitness: Arctic & Antarctic. DK Publishing, 1996.

National Geographic's Arctic Kingdom: Life at the Edge. National Geographic, 1998.

Websites

<http://www.arctic-travel.com>

<http://www.civilization.ca/membrs /canhist/frobisher/frint01e.html>

<http://www.geographic.org/flags /nunavut_flags.html>

<http://www.gov.nu.ca>

<http://www.pbs.org/wnet/nature /toothwalkers/index.html>

Organizations

Nunavut Tourism
P.O. Box 1450
Iqaluit, NT X0A 0H0
Canada
Tel: (867) 979-6551 or (800) 491-7910
Fax: (867) 979-1261
E-mail: <nunatour@nunanet.com>
Website: <http://www.nunatour.nt.ca>

Press Secretary
Office of the Premier
Grinnell Place
P.O. Box 800
Iqaluit, NT X0A 0H0
Tel: (867) 979-5822
Fax: (867) 979-5833
E-mail: <abourgeois@gov.nu.ca>

INDEX

ABOUT THE AUTHOR

Danielle Corriveau was raised on the Barrengrounds in the ways of her Inuit ancestors. Later, her family's wanderings brought her to the Upper Great Lakes and to modern Western society. She lives and works in Ontario, Canada, as a writer and artist, translating her experiences with the "outside" world for other Inuit and explaining the old Inuit ways of life to non-Inuit. She also writes a column on aboriginal issues and Arctic history for *Nunatsiaq News*, Nunavut's territorial newspaper.

PICTURE CREDITS

(B=bottom; C=center; F=far; I=inset; L=left; M=main; R=right; T=top)

ANA Press Agency: 25T, 29IT, 29IC, 35T • Archive Photos: 15C, 15I, 16L, 16–17M, 17T, 18L, 18–19M, 19I, 23T, 22–23M • Bes Stock: 36L • Camera Press: 3, 4, 5B, 12T, 12C, 27R, 34L • Claus Lotscher: 13T • Focus Team—Italy: 26L, 27T • Gerry Kruschenske: cover • John Elk III: 2 • Nik Wheeler: 41B • Nunavut Tourism: 15T, 21T • Robert Semeniuk: 6–7M, 7T, 8–9M, 10FL, 10B, 21I, 24–25M, 30–31M, 34–35M, 35I, 37T • Still Pictures: 24L • Sylvia Cordaiy: 8L, 9I • Tessa Macintosh: 20L, 23B, 25R, 30L, 31T, 32L, 38–39M, 39C, 40–41M • Topham Picturepoint: 20–21M, 32–33M, 39T, 44–45M • Trip Photographic Library: 14–15M, 26–27M • Winnipeg Art Gallery: 43T • Winston Fraser: 11I, 29CL, 42–43M, 45T, 45B • Yvette Cardozo: title page, 7I, 9T, 10–11M, 11T, 12–13M, 14L, 28L, 28–29M, 29IB, 31B, 33T, 33C, 36–37M, 37B, 39I, 42L, 46, 47